family favorites
chocolate

Bath · New York · Singapore · Hong Kong · Cologne · Delhi · Melbourne

boston crème pie

ingredients

SERVES 6

8 oz/225 g ready-prepared
    pie dough

filling

3 eggs

4 oz/115 g/scant $^2/_3$ cup
    superfine sugar

5 oz/150 g/generous $^3/_8$ cup
    all-purpose flour, plus
    extra for dusting

1 tbsp confectioners' sugar

pinch of salt

1 tsp vanilla extract

14 fl oz/400 ml/1$^3/_4$ cups milk

5 fl oz/150 ml/$^2/_3$ cup
    plain yogurt

5$^1/_2$ oz/150 g semisweet
    chocolate, broken into
    pieces

2 tbsp Kirsch

to decorate

5 fl oz/150 ml/$^2/_3$ cup
    sour cream

8 oz/225 g semisweet
    chocolate shavings
    or caraque

method

1 Roll out the pie dough and use to line a 9-inch/23-cm loose-bottom tart pan. Prick the base with a fork, line with parchment paper, and fill with dried beans. Bake in a preheated oven, 400°F/200°C, for 20 minutes. Remove the beans and paper and return the pastry shell to the oven for an additional 5 minutes. Remove from the oven and place on a wire rack to cool.

2 To make the filling, beat the eggs and superfine sugar in a heatproof bowl until fluffy. Sift in the flour, confectioners' sugar, and salt. Stir in the vanilla extract.

3 Bring the milk and yogurt to a boil in a small pan and strain it over the egg mixture. Set the bowl over a pan of barely simmering water. Stir the custard until it coats the back of a spoon.

4 Gently heat the chocolate with the Kirsch in a separate small pan until the chocolate has melted. Stir into the custard. Remove from the heat and stand the bowl in cold water. Let cool.

5 Pour the chocolate mixture into the pastry shell. Spread the sour cream evenly over the chocolate and decorate with chocolate shavings or caraque.

chocolate meringue pie

ingredients

SERVES 6

8 oz/225 g semisweet
   chocolate graham
   crackers
4 tbsp butter

filling

3 egg yolks
4 tbsp superfine sugar
4 tbsp cornstarch
1 pint/600 ml/2$\frac{1}{2}$ cups milk
3$\frac{1}{2}$ oz/100 g semisweet
   chocolate, melted

meringue

2 egg whites
3$\frac{1}{2}$ oz/100 g/$\frac{1}{2}$ cup
   superfine sugar
$\frac{1}{4}$ tsp vanilla extract

method

1 Place the crackers in a plastic bag and crush with a rolling pin, then transfer to a large bowl. Place the butter in a small, heavy-bottom pan and heat gently until just melted, then stir it into the cracker crumbs until well mixed. Press into the bottom and up the sides of a 9-inch/23-cm tart pan or dish.

2 To make the filling, place the egg yolks, superfine sugar, and cornstarch in a large bowl and beat until they form a smooth paste, adding a little of the milk, if necessary. Place the milk into a small, heavy-bottom pan and heat gently until almost boiling, then slowly pour it onto the egg mixture, whisking well.

3 Return the mixture to the pan and cook gently, whisking, until thick. Remove from the heat. Whisk in the melted chocolate, then pour it onto the cracker base.

4 To make the meringue, whisk the egg whites in a large, spotlessly clean, greasefree bowl until soft peaks form. Gradually whisk in two-thirds of the sugar until the mixture is stiff and glossy. Fold in the remaining sugar and vanilla extract.

5 Spread the meringue over the filling, swirling the surface with the back of a spoon to give it an attractive finish. Bake in the center of a preheated oven, 375°F/160°C, for 30 minutes, or until golden. Serve hot or just warm.

pecan & chocolate pie

ingredients

SERVES 6–8

pie dough

6 oz/175 g/scant 1/2 cup
    all-purpose flour, plus
    extra for dusting

3 1/2 oz /100 g butter, diced

1 tbsp golden superfine sugar

1 egg yolk, beaten with
    1 tbsp water

filling

2 oz/55 g butter

3 tbsp unsweetened cocoa

8 fl oz/225 ml/1 cup
    corn syrup

3 eggs

2 1/2 oz/70 g/3/8 cup firmly
    packed dark brown sugar

6 oz/175 g/3/4 cup shelled
    pecans, chopped

to serve

whipped cream

ground cinnamon,
    for dusting

method

1 To make the pie dough, sift the flour into a large bowl. Rub in the butter until the mixture resembles fine bread crumbs, then stir in the superfine sugar. Stir in the beaten egg yolk. Knead lightly to form a firm dough, cover with plastic wrap, and let chill in the refrigerator for 1 1/2 hours. Roll out the chilled dough on a lightly floured counter and use it to line an 8-inch/20-cm tart pan.

2 To make the filling, place the butter in a small, heavy-bottom pan and heat gently until melted. Sift in the cocoa and stir in the syrup. Place the eggs and sugar in a large bowl and beat together. Add the syrup mixture and the chopped pecans and stir. Pour the mixture into the prepared pastry shell.

3 Place the pie on a preheated cookie sheet and bake in a preheated oven, 375°F/190°C, for 35–40 minutes, or until the filling is just set. Let cool slightly and serve warm with a spoonful of whipped cream, dusted with ground cinnamon.

mississippi mud pie

ingredients

SERVES 8

pie dough

8 oz/225 g/scant 1⅝ cups
    all-purpose flour, plus
    extra for dusting
2 tbsp unsweetened cocoa
5½ oz/150 g butter
2 tbsp superfine sugar
1–2 tbsp cold water

filling

6 oz/175 g butter
12 oz/350 g/scant 1¾ cups
    packed brown sugar
4 eggs, lightly beaten
4 tbsp unsweetened cocoa,
    sifted
5½ oz/150 g semisweet
    chocolate
10 fl oz/300 ml/1¼ cups
    light cream
1 tsp chocolate extract

to decorate

15 fl oz/425 ml/scant 2 cups
    heavy cream, whipped
chocolate flakes and curls

method

1 To make the pie dough, sift the flour and cocoa into a mixing bowl. Rub in the butter with the fingertips until the mixture resembles fine bread crumbs. Stir in the sugar and enough cold water to mix to a soft dough. Wrap the dough and let chill in the refrigerator for 15 minutes.

2 Roll out the dough on a lightly floured counter and use to line a 9-inch/23-cm loose-bottom tart pan or ceramic pie dish. Line with parchment paper and fill with dried beans. Bake in a preheated oven, 375°F/190°C, for 15 minutes. Remove from the oven and take out the paper and beans. Bake the pastry shell for an additional 10 minutes.

3 To make the filling, beat the butter and sugar together in a bowl and gradually beat in the eggs with the cocoa. Melt the chocolate and beat it into the mixture with the light cream and the chocolate extract.

4 Reduce the oven temperature to 325°F/160°C. Pour the mixture into the pastry shell and bake for 45 minutes, or until the filling has set gently.

5 Let the mud pie cool completely, then transfer it to a serving plate, if you like. Cover with the whipped cream. Decorate the pie with chocolate flakes and curls and then let chill until ready to serve.

chocolate crumble pie

ingredients

SERVES 8

pie dough

7 oz/200 g/scant 1¹/₄ cups
   all-purpose flour
1 tsp baking powder
4 oz/115 g unsalted butter,
   cut into small pieces
1 oz/25 g/generous ¹/₄ cup
   superfine sugar
1 egg yolk
1–2 tsp cold water

filling

5 fl oz/150 ml/²/₃ cup
   heavy cream
5 fl oz/150 ml/²/₃ cup milk
8 oz/225 g semisweet
   chocolate, chopped
2 eggs

crumble topping

3¹/₂ oz/100 g/generous
   ¹/₂ cup packed
   brown sugar
3 oz/85 g/³/₄ cup
   toasted pecans
4 oz/115 g semisweet
   chocolate
3 oz/85 g amaretti cookies
1 tsp unsweetened cocoa

method

1 To make the pie dough, sift the flour and baking powder into a large bowl, rub in the butter, and stir in the sugar, then add the egg and a little water to bring the dough together. Turn the dough out, and knead briefly. Wrap the dough and let chill in the refrigerator for 30 minutes.

2 Preheat the oven to 375°F/190°C. Roll out the pie dough and use to line a 9-inch/23-cm loose-bottom tart pan. Prick the pastry shell with a fork. Line with parchment paper and fill with dried beans. Bake in the oven for 15 minutes. Remove from the oven and take out the paper and beans. Reduce the oven temperature to 350°F/180°C.

3 Bring the cream and milk to a boil in a pan, remove from the heat, and add the chocolate. Stir until melted and smooth. Beat the eggs and add to the chocolate mixture, mix thoroughly and pour into the shell. Bake for 15 minutes, remove from the oven, and let rest for 1 hour.

4 When you are ready to serve the pie, place the topping ingredients in the food processor and pulse to chop. (If you do not have a processor, place the sugar in a large bowl, chop the nuts and chocolate with a large knife, and crush the cookies, then add to the bowl with the cocoa and mix well.) Sprinkle over the pie, then serve it in slices.

hot chocolate cheesecake

ingredients

SERVES 8

butter, for greasing

pie dough

5 1/2 oz/150 g/generous 1 cup
    all-purpose flour

2 tbsp unsweetened cocoa

2 3/4 oz/75 g butter, diced

2 tbsp golden superfine sugar

1 oz/25 g/1/4 cup ground
    almonds

1 egg yolk

filling

2 eggs, separated

2 3/4 oz/75 g/scant 3/8 cup
    golden superfine sugar

12 oz/350 g/1 1/2 cups
    cream cheese

1 1/2 oz/40 g/3/8 cup
    ground almonds

5 fl oz/150 ml/2/3 cup
    heavy cream

1 oz/25 g/1/4 cup
    unsweetened
    cocoa, sifted

1 tsp vanilla extract

confectioners' sugar,
    for dusting

method

1 To make the pie dough, sift the flour and unsweetened cocoa into a bowl. Add the butter and rub it in until the mixture resembles fine bread crumbs. Stir in the sugar and almonds. Add the egg yolk and enough water to make a soft dough. Roll out on a lightly floured counter and use to line an 8-inch/20-cm loose-bottom cake pan greased with butter. Let chill in the refrigerator while preparing the filling.

2 To make the filling, place the egg yolks and superfine sugar in a large bowl and whisk together until thick and pale. Whisk in the cheese, almonds, cream, cocoa, and vanilla extract until blended.

3 Place the egg whites in a clean, greasefree bowl and whisk until stiff but not dry. Stir a little of the whisked egg whites into the cheese mixture, then fold in the remainder. Pour into the pastry shell. Bake in a preheated oven, 325°F/160°C, for 1 1/2 hours, or until risen and just firm to the touch. Remove from the pan and dust with confectioners' sugar.

chocolate bread pudding

ingredients

SERVES 4

6 thick slices white bread, crusts removed

16 fl oz/450 ml/scant 2 cups milk

6 fl oz/175 ml canned evaporated milk

2 tbsp unsweetened cocoa

2 eggs

2 tbsp brown sugar

1 tsp vanilla extract

confectioners' sugar, for dusting

hot fudge sauce

2 oz/55 g semisweet chocolate, broken into pieces

1 tbsp unsweetened cocoa

2 tbsp light corn syrup

2 oz/55 g/$^1/_4$ cup butter or margarine

2 tbsp brown sugar

5 fl oz/150 ml/$^2/_3$ cup milk

1 tbsp cornstarch

method

1 Grease a shallow ovenproof dish. Cut the bread into squares and layer them in the dish.

2 Put the milk, evaporated milk, and the unsweetened cocoa in a pan and heat gently, stirring occasionally, until the mixture is lukewarm. Whisk the eggs, sugar, and vanilla extract together. Add the warm milk mixture and beat well.

3 Pour into the prepared dish, making sure that all the bread is completely covered. Cover the dish with plastic wrap and let chill in the refrigerator for 1–2 hours, then bake in a preheated oven 350°F/180°C, for 35–40 minutes, until set. Let stand for 5 minutes.

4 To make the sauce, put all the ingredients into a pan and heat gently, stirring constantly until smooth.

5 Dust the chocolate bread pudding with confectioners' sugar and serve immediately with the hot fudge sauce.

rich chocolate ice cream

ingredients

SERVES 6
ice cream

1 egg

3 egg yolks

3 oz/85 g/scant $^1/_2$ cup
    superfine sugar

10 fl oz/300 ml/$1^1/_4$ cups
    whole milk

9 oz/250 g semisweet
    chocolate

10 fl oz/250 g/$1^1/_4$ cups
    heavy cream

trellis cups
$3^1/_2$ oz/100 g semisweet
    chocolate

method

1 Beat the egg, egg yolks, and superfine sugar together in a mixing bowl until well combined. Heat the milk until it is almost boiling. Gradually pour the hot milk onto the eggs, whisking. Place the bowl over a pan of gently simmering water and cook, stirring constantly, until the custard mixture thickens sufficiently to thinly coat the back of a wooden spoon.

2 Break the chocolate into small pieces and add to the hot custard. Stir until the chocolate has melted. Cover with a sheet of dampened baking parchment and let cool.

3 Whip the cream until just holding its shape, then fold into the cooled chocolate custard. Transfer to a freezerproof container and freeze for 1–2 hours until the mixture is frozen 1 inch/2.5 cm from the sides. Scrape the ice cream into a chilled bowl and beat again until smooth. Re-freeze until firm.

4 To make the trellis cups, invert a muffin pan and cover 6 alternate mounds with plastic wrap. Melt the chocolate, place it in a paper pastry bag, and snip off the end.

5 Pipe a circle around the bottom of the mound, then pipe chocolate back and forth over it to form a double-thickness trellis. Pipe around the bottom again. Chill until set, then lift from the pan and remove the plastic wrap. Serve the ice cream in the trellis cups.

marble cheesecake

ingredients

SERVES 10

base

8 oz/225 g toasted oat cereal

1³/₄ oz/50 g/¹/₂ cup toasted
    hazelnuts, chopped

4 tbsp butter

1 oz/25 g semisweet chocolate

filling

12 oz/350 g full-fat soft cheese

3¹/₂ oz/100 g/¹/₂ cup
    superfine sugar

7 fl oz/200 ml/generous
    ³/₄ cup thick yogurt

10 fl oz/300 ml/1¹/₄ cups
    heavy cream

1 packaged powdered gelatin

3 tbsp water

6 oz/175 g semisweet
    chocolate, melted

6 oz/175 g white chocolate,
    melted

method

1 Place the toasted oat cereal in a plastic bag and crush it coarsely with a rolling pin. Pour the crushed cereal into a mixing bowl and stir in the toasted chopped hazelnuts.

2 Melt the butter and chocolate together over low heat and stir into the cereal mixture, stirring until well coated.

3 Using the bottom of a glass, press the mixture into the bottom and up the sides of an 8-inch/ 20-cm springform cake pan.

4 Beat the cheese and sugar together with a wooden spoon until smooth. Beat in the yogurt. Whip the cream until just holding its shape and fold into the mixture. Sprinkle the gelatin over the water in a heatproof bowl and let it go spongy. Place over a pan of hot water and stir until dissolved. Stir into the mixture.

5 Divide the mixture in half and beat the semisweet chocolate into one half and the white chocolate into the other half.

6 Place alternate spoonfuls of mixture on top of the cereal base. Swirl the filling together with the tip of a knife to give a marbled effect. Smooth the top with a scraper or a spatula. Chill the cheesecake for at least 2 hours, until set, before serving.

chocolate marshmallow cake

ingredients

SERVES 6

6 tbsp unsalted butter

8 oz/225 g/generous 1 cup
    superfine sugar

$^1/_2$ tsp vanilla extract

2 eggs, beaten lightly

3 oz/85 g semisweet chocolate,
    broken into pieces

5 fl oz/150 ml/$^2/_3$ cup
    buttermilk

6 oz/175 g/1$^1/_4$ cups
    self-rising flour

$^1/_2$ tsp baking soda

pinch of salt

frosting

6 oz/175 g white
    marshmallows

1 tbsp milk

2 egg whites

2 tbsp superfine sugar

2 oz/55 g light chocolate,
    grated, to decorate

method

1 Cream the butter, sugar, and vanilla together in a bowl until pale and fluffy, then gradually beat in the eggs.

2 Melt the chocolate in a bowl over a pan of simmering water. Stir in the buttermilk gradually until well combined. Let cool slightly.

3 Sift the flour, baking soda, and salt into a separate bowl. Add the chocolate and the flour mixtures alternately to the creamed mixture, a little at a time. Spoon the mixture into a greased 1$^1/_2$-pint/850-ml/3$^1/_3$-cup ovenproof bowl greased with butter and smooth the surface. Bake in a preheated oven, 325°F/160°C, for 50 minutes until a skewer inserted into the center of the cake comes out clean. Turn out onto a wire rack to cool.

4 Meanwhile, make the frosting. Heat the marshmallows and milk very gently in a small pan until the marshmallows have melted. Remove from the heat and let cool. Whisk the egg whites until soft peaks form, then add the sugar and continue whisking, until stiff peaks form. Fold into the cooled marshmallow mixture and set aside for 10 minutes.

5 When the cake is cool, cover the top and sides with the marshmallow frosting. Top with grated light chocolate.

double chocolate roulade

ingredients

SERVES 8

4 eggs, separated

4 oz/115 g/generous $\frac{1}{2}$ cup
 golden superfine sugar

4 oz/115 g semisweet
 chocolate, melted
 and cooled

1 tsp instant coffee granules,
 dissolved in 2 tbsp hot
 water, cooled

confectioners' sugar,
 to decorate

unsweetened cocoa,
 for dusting

fresh raspberries, to serve

filling

9 fl oz/250 ml/generous 1 cup
 whipping cream

5 oz/140 g white chocolate,
 broken into pieces

3 tbsp Tia Maria

method

1 Line a 9 x 13-inch/23 x 33-cm jelly roll pan with nonstick parchment paper. Whisk the egg yolks and sugar in a bowl until pale and mousse-like. Fold in the chocolate, then the coffee. Place the egg whites in a clean bowl and whisk until stiff but not dry. Stir a little of the egg whites into the chocolate mixture, then fold in the remainder. Pour into the pan and bake in a preheated oven, 350°F/180°C, for 15–20 minutes, or until firm. Cover with a damp dish towel and let stand in the pan for 8 hours, or overnight.

2 Meanwhile, make the filling. Heat the cream until almost boiling. Place the chocolate in a food processor and chop coarsely. With the motor running, pour the cream through the feed tube. Process until smooth. Stir in the Tia Maria. Transfer to a bowl and let cool. Let chill for 8 hours, or overnight.

3 To assemble the roulade, whip the chocolate cream until soft peaks form. Cut a sheet of waxed paper larger than the roulade, place on a counter and sift confectioners' sugar over it. Turn the roulade out onto the paper. Peel away the lining paper. Spread the chocolate cream over the roulade and roll up from the short side nearest to you. Transfer to a dish, seam-side down. Let chill for 2 hours, then dust with cocoa. Serve with raspberries.

mocha layer cake

ingredients

SERVES 8

butter for greasing

7 oz/200 g/generous
    1¼ cups self-rising flour

¼ tsp baking powder

4 tbsp unsweetened cocoa

3½ oz/100 g/ ½ cup
    superfine sugar

2 eggs

2 tbsp corn syrup

5 fl oz/150 ml/⅔ cup corn oil

5 fl oz/150 ml/⅔ cup milk

filling

1 tsp instant coffee

1 tbsp boiling water

10 fl oz/300 ml/1¼ cups
    heavy cream

2 tbsp confectioners' sugar

to decorate

1¾ oz/50 g semisweet
    chocolate, grated

chocolate caraque

confectioners' sugar,
    for dusting

method

1 Sift the flour, baking powder, and cocoa into a large bowl, then stir in the sugar. Make a well in the center and stir in the eggs, syrup, corn oil, and milk. Beat with a wooden spoon, gradually mixing in the dry ingredients to make a smooth batter. Divide the mixture between 3 lightly greased 3 x 7-inch/18-cm cake pans.

2 Bake in a preheated oven, 350°F/180°C, for 35–45 minutes, or until springy to the touch. Let stand in the pans for 5 minutes, then turn out and let cool completely on a wire rack.

3 To make the filling, dissolve the instant coffee in the boiling water and place in a large bowl with the cream and confectioners' sugar. Whip until the cream is just holding its shape, then use half the cream to sandwich the 3 cakes together. Spread the remaining cream over the top and sides of the cake. Press the grated chocolate into the cream round the edge of the cake.

4 Transfer the cake to a serving plate. Lay the chocolate caraque over the top of the cake. Cut a few thin strips of parchment paper and place on top of the chocolate caraque. Dust lightly with confectioners' sugar, then carefully remove the paper. Serve.

chocolate passion cake

ingredients

SERVES 6

butter, for greasing

5 eggs

5 1/2 oz/150 g/generous
  3/4 cup superfine sugar

5 1/2 oz/150 g/1 cup
  all-purpose flour

1 1/2 oz/40 g/generous 3/8 cup
  unsweetened cocoa

6 oz/175 g carrots, peeled,
  finely grated, and
  squeezed until dry

1 3/4 oz/50 g/generous 3/8 cup
  chopped walnuts

2 tbsp corn oil

12 oz/350 g/1 1/2 cups
  medium-fat soft cheese

6 oz/175 g/1 1/2 cups
  confectioners' sugar

6 oz/175 g milk or semisweet
  chocolate, melted

method

1 Place the eggs and sugar in a large bowl set over a pan of gently simmering water and, using an electric whisk, whisk until the mixture is very thick and the whisk leaves a trail that lasts a few seconds when lifted.

2 Remove the bowl from the heat. Sift the flour and cocoa into the bowl and carefully fold in. Fold in the carrots, walnuts, and corn oil until the cake batter is just blended.

3 Pour into a lightly greased and base-lined 8-inch/20-cm deep round cake pan and bake in a preheated oven, 375°F/190°C, for 45 minutes. Let cool slightly, then turn out onto a wire rack to cool completely.

4 Beat the soft cheese and confectioners' sugar together until blended, then beat in the melted chocolate. Split the cake in half and sandwich together again with half the chocolate mixture. Cover the top of the cake with the remainder of the chocolate mixture, swirling it with a knife. Let chill in the refrigerator or serve immediately.

family chocolate cake

ingredients

SERVES 8

4 1/2 oz/125 g/1/2 cup soft
    margarine

4 1/2 oz/125 g/1/2 cup
    superfine sugar

2 eggs

1 tbsp light corn syrup

4 1/2 oz/125 g/1 cup self-rising
    flour, sifted

2 tbsp unsweetened cocoa,
    sifted

filling and topping

4 tbsp confectioners' sugar,
    sifted

2 tbsp butter

3 1/2 oz/100 g white or light
    cooking chocolate

a little light or white chocolate,
    melted (optional)

method

1 Place all of the ingredients for the cake in a large mixing bowl and beat with a wooden spoon or electric mixer to form a smooth mixture.

2 Divide the mixture between 2 lightly greased 7-inch/18-cm shallow cake pans and smooth the tops. Bake in a preheated oven, 375°F/190°C, for 20 minutes or until springy to the touch. Cool for a few minutes in the pans then transfer to a wire rack to cool completely.

3 To make the filling, beat the sugar and butter together in a bowl until light and fluffy. Melt the white or light cooking chocolate and beat half into the icing mixture. Use the filling to sandwich the 2 cakes together.

4 Spread the remaining melted cooking chocolate over the top of the cake. Pipe circles of contrasting light or white chocolate and feather into the cooking chocolate with a toothpick, if desired. Let the cake set before serving.

cappuccino squares

ingredients

MAKES 15

8 oz/225 g butter, softened, plus extra for greasing

8 oz/225 g/generous 1 1/2 cups self-rising flour

1 tsp baking powder

1 tsp unsweetened cocoa, plus extra for dusting

8 oz/225 g/generous 1 cup golden superfine sugar

4 eggs, beaten

3 tbsp instant coffee powder, dissolved in 2 tbsp hot water

white chocolate frosting

4 oz/115 g white chocolate, broken into pieces

2 oz/55 g butter, softened

3 tbsp milk

6 oz/175 g/1 3/4 cups confectioners' sugar

method

1 Sift the flour, baking powder, and cocoa into a bowl and add the butter, superfine sugar, eggs, and coffee. Beat well, by hand or with an electric whisk, until smooth, then spoon into a greased and base-lined shallow 11 x 7-inch/ 28 x 18-cm pan and smooth the top.

2 Bake in a preheated oven, 350°F/180°C, for 35–40 minutes, or until risen and firm, then turn out onto a wire rack and peel off the lining paper. Let cool completely. To make the frosting, place the chocolate, butter, and milk in a bowl set over a pan of simmering water and stir until the chocolate has melted.

3 Remove the bowl from the pan and sift in the confectioners' sugar. Beat until smooth, then spread over the cake. Dust the top of the cake with sifted cocoa, then cut into squares.

mocha brownies

ingredients

MAKES 16

2 oz/55 g butter, plus extra for greasing

4 oz/115 g semisweet chocolate, broken into pieces

6 oz/175 g/scant 1 cup brown sugar

2 eggs

1 tbsp instant coffee powder dissolved in 1 tbsp hot water, cooled

3 oz/85 g/scant $^2/_3$ cup all-purpose flour

$^1/_2$ tsp baking powder

2 oz/55 g/$^1/_3$ cup coarsely chopped pecans

method

1 Place the chocolate and butter in a heavy-bottom pan over low heat until melted. Stir and let cool.

2 Place the sugar and eggs in a large bowl and cream together until light and fluffy. Fold in the chocolate mixture and cooled coffee and mix thoroughly. Sift in the flour and baking powder and lightly fold into the mixture, then carefully fold in the pecans.

3 Pour the batter into a greased and base-lined 8-inch/20-cm square cake pan and bake in a preheated oven, 350°F/180°C, for 25–30 minutes, or until firm and a skewer inserted into the center comes out clean.

4 Let cool in the pan for a few minutes, then run a knife round the edge of the cake to loosen it. Turn the cake out onto a wire rack and peel off the lining paper. Let cool completely. When cold, cut into squares.

caramel chocolate shortbread

ingredients

MAKES 24

4 oz/115 g butter, plus extra
　　for greasing
6 oz/175 g/³/₄ cup plain flour
2 oz/55 g/¹/₃ cup golden
　　superfine sugar

filling and topping

6 oz/175 g butter
4 oz/115 g/²/₃ cup golden
　　superfine sugar
3 tbsp corn syrup
14 oz/400 g canned
　　condensed milk
7 oz/200 g plain chocolate,
　　broken into pieces

method

1 Place the butter, flour and sugar in a food processor and process until it begins to bind together. Press the mixture into a greased and base-lined 23-cm/9-inch shallow square cake tin and smooth the top. Bake in a preheated oven, 350°F/180°C, for 20–25 minutes, or until golden.

2 Meanwhile, make the filling. Place the butter, sugar, syrup and condensed milk in a saucepan and heat gently until the sugar has melted. Bring to the boil and simmer for 6–8 minutes, stirring constantly, until the mixture becomes very thick. Pour over the shortbread base and leave to chill in the refrigerator until firm.

3 To make the topping, melt the chocolate and leave to cool, then spread over the caramel. Chill in the refrigerator until set. Cut the shortbread into 12 pieces with a sharp knife and serve.

chocolate butter cookies

ingredients

SERVES 4

3$\frac{1}{2}$ oz/100 g butter, softened,
    plus extra for greasing

3$\frac{1}{2}$ oz/100 g/$\frac{1}{2}$ cup
    superfine sugar

1 egg yolk

8 oz/225 g/1$\frac{1}{2}$ cups
    all-purpose flour, sifted,
    plus extra for dusting

about 2 tbsp milk

frosting

9 oz/250 g/scant 1$\frac{1}{2}$ cups
    confectioners' sugar, sifted

1 tbsp unsweetened cocoa
    powder

about 3 tbsp orange juice

method

1 Put the butter and all but a tablespoon of the sugar into a large bowl and cream until pale and fluffy. Beat in the egg yolk, then add the flour and mix well. Stir in enough milk to form a smooth dough.

2 Roll out the dough on a lightly floured work surface. Cut out rounds using a 3-inch/7.5-cm cookie cutter. Arrange the circles on 2 large, greased cookie sheets, leaving enough space between them to allow them to spread during cooking. Sprinkle over the remaining sugar and bake in a preheated oven, 400°F/200°C, for 15 minutes, or until golden. Remove the cookies from the oven, transfer to wire racks, and let cool completely.

3 To make the frosting, put the confectioners' sugar and cocoa powder into a bowl. Stir in the orange juice gradually until enough has been added to make a thin frosting. Put a teaspoonful of frosting on each cookie and let set before serving.

chocolate chip oaties

ingredients

MAKES ABOUT 20

4 oz/115 g butter, softened,
    plus extra for greasing

4 oz/115 g/$^{1}/_{2}$ cup firmly
    packed light brown sugar

1 egg

3$^{1}/_{2}$ oz/100 g/1 cup
    rolled oats

1 tbsp milk

1 tsp vanilla extract

4$^{1}/_{2}$ oz/125 g/scant 1 cup
    all-purpose flour

1 tbsp unsweetened cocoa

$^{1}/_{2}$ tsp baking powder

6 oz/175 g semisweet
    chocolate, broken
    into pieces

6 oz/175 g milk chocolate,
    broken into pieces

method

1 Place the butter and sugar in a bowl and beat together until light and fluffy. Beat in the egg, then add the oats, milk, and vanilla extract. Beat together until well blended. Sift the flour, unsweetened cocoa, and baking powder into the cookie batter and stir. Stir in the chocolate pieces.

2 Place dessertspoonfuls of the cookie batter on 2 greased cookie sheets and flatten slightly with a fork. Bake in a preheated oven, 350°F/180°C, for 15 minutes, or until slightly risen and firm. Let cool on the cookie sheets for 2 minutes, then transfer to wire racks to cool completely.

mocha walnut cookies

ingredients

MAKES ABOUT 16

4 oz/115 g butter, softened,
   plus extra for greasing
4 oz/115 g/$1/2$ cup firmly
   packed light brown sugar
3 oz/85 g/$3/8$ cup golden
   granulated sugar
1 tsp vanilla extract
1 tbsp instant coffee
   granules, dissolved in
   1 tbsp hot water
1 egg
6oz/175 g/1 cup
   all-purpose flour
$1/2$ tsp baking powder
$1/4$ tsp baking soda
2 oz/55 g/$1/3$ cup milk
   chocolate chips
2 oz/55 g/$1/4$ cup shelled
   walnuts, coarsely chopped

method

1 Place the butter, brown sugar, and granulated sugar in a large mixing bowl and beat together thoroughly until light and fluffy. Place the vanilla extract, coffee, and egg in a separate bowl and whisk together.

2 Gradually add the coffee mixture to the butter and sugar, beating until fluffy. Sift the flour, baking powder, and baking soda into the cookie batter and fold in carefully. Fold in the chocolate chips and walnuts.

3 Place dessertspoonfuls of the cookie batter onto 2 greased cookie sheets, allowing room for the cookies to spread. Bake in a preheated oven, 350°F/180°C, for 10–15 minutes, or until crisp on the outside but still soft inside. Let cool on the cookie sheets for 2 minutes, then transfer to wire racks and let cool completely.

ladies kisses

ingredients

MAKES 20

5 oz/140 g unsalted butter

4 oz/115 g/generous $1/2$ cup
superfine sugar

1 egg yolk

4 oz/115 g/generous 1 cup
ground almonds

6 oz/175 g/generous 1 cup
all-purpose flour

2 oz/55 g semisweet
chocolate, broken
into pieces

2 tbsp confectioners' sugar

2 tbsp unsweetened cocoa

method

1 Beat the butter and sugar together in a bowl until pale and fluffy. Beat in the egg yolk, then beat in the almonds and flour. Continue beating until well mixed. Shape the dough into a ball, wrap in plastic wrap, and let chill in the refrigerator for $11/2$–2 hours.

2 Unwrap the dough, break off walnut-size pieces, and roll them into balls between the palms of your hands. Place the dough balls on 3 cookie sheets lined with parchment paper, allowing room for expansion during cooking. Bake in a preheated oven, 325°F/160°C, for 20–25 minutes, or until golden brown. Carefully transfer the cookies, still on the parchment paper, if using, to wire racks to cool.

3 Place the semisweet chocolate in a small heatproof bowl and set over a pan of barely simmering water, stirring constantly, until melted. Remove the bowl from the heat.

4 Remove the cookies from the parchment paper, if using, and spread the melted chocolate over the bases. Sandwich them together in pairs and return to the wire racks to cool. Dust with a mixture of confectioners' sugar and cocoa and serve.

chocolate viennese fingers

ingredients

MAKES ABOUT 30

4 oz/115 g butter, softened,
    plus extra for greasing
2 oz/55 g/$\frac{1}{2}$ cup golden
    confectioners' sugar, sifted
$4\frac{1}{2}$ oz/125 g/generous
    $\frac{3}{4}$ cup all-purpose flour
1 tbsp unsweetened cocoa
$3\frac{1}{2}$ oz/100 g semisweet
    chocolate, melted
    and cooled

method

1 Beat the butter and sugar together until light and fluffy. Sift the flour and unsweetened cocoa into the bowl and work the mixture until it is a smooth, piping consistency.

2 Spoon into a large pastry bag fitted with a 1-inch/2.5-cm fluted tip. Pipe $2\frac{1}{2}$-inch/6-cm lengths of the mixture onto 2 greased cookie sheets, allowing room for expansion during cooking. Bake in a preheated oven, 350°F/180°C, for 15 minutes, or until firm.

3 Let cool on the cookie sheets for 2 minutes, then transfer to a wire rack to cool completely. Dip the ends of the cookies into the melted chocolate and let set before serving.

done 09-04-09

easy chocolate fudge

ingredients

MAKES 25 PIECES

2³/₄ oz/75 g unsalted butter,
   cut into even-size pieces,
   plus extra for greasing

1 lb 2 oz/500 g semisweet
   chocolate

14 oz/400 g canned sweetened
   condensed milk

¹/₂ tsp vanilla extract

method

1 Lightly grease an 8-inch/20-cm square cake pan with butter. Break the chocolate into small pieces and place in a large, heavy-bottom pan with the butter and condensed milk.

2 Heat gently, stirring constantly, until the chocolate and butter melt and the mixture is smooth. Do not let boil. Remove from the heat. Beat in the vanilla extract, then beat the mixture for a few minutes until thickened. Pour it into the pan and level the top.

3 Let the mixture chill in the refrigerator for 1 hour, or until firm. Tip the fudge out onto a cutting board and cut into squares to serve.

for a richer fudge
Use ¹/₂ milk choc 2 ³/₄
¹/₂ semi sweet 2 ⁶/₄
+ 1 ³/₄
———
5 ¹/₂ oz.